Benjamin Britten

Two Psalms
Out of the deep, Praise ye the Lord

for SATB chorus and orchestra

Vocal Score

CHESTER MUSIC

CH79761

© The Britten Estate Ltd
Worldwide publication rights licensed to Chester Music Limited, 2013

Head office:
14–15, Berners Street,
London W1T 3LJ
England

Tel +44 (0)20 7612 7400
Fax +44 (0)20 7612 7549

Sales and hire:
Music Sales Distribution Centre,
Newmarket Road,
Bury St Edmunds,
Suffolk IP33 3YB
England

Tel +44 (0)1284 702600
Fax +44 (0)1284 768301

www.musicsalesclassical.com

Keyboard reduction by Hywel Davies

Full score and orchestral parts are available for hire from the publisher.

Preface

The Two Psalms are remarkable examples of an important period in Britten's development. Their story begins on 8 July 1931, the date he began to draft the first of the pair, Psalm 130 ('Out of the deep have I call'd unto thee, O Lord'). His initial thoughts, recorded that very day, are not positive ('Practise in morning as usual, & also begin a mediocre setting of Psalm 130. . .'); however, encouragement from his composition teacher at the time, John Ireland, instilled greater enthusiasm for the piece and by 3 October in the same year he was 'quite bucked with it'. A companion piece, Psalm 150 ('Praise ye the Lord'), was begun four days later on 7 October.

These large-scale choral pieces, with full orchestral accompaniment covering eighty-two sides of manuscript paper, are among the most substantial compositions from Britten's time studying at the Royal College of Music (1930-1933). Other orchestral works from 1931 include a setting of Three Small Songs and the ballet *Plymouth Town*, both for small orchestra; the choral works of the same period, such as *Thy King's Birthday* (published as *Christ's Nativity*) and Variations on a French Carol, were unaccompanied. In fact, in terms of the scale of ambition, the Psalms hark back to Britten's earlier years, particularly the period 1926-1927, when he was given to grandly dashing off symphonies, tone poems, fantasias and complete mass settings—the manuscripts of which were often completed from scratch in a matter of days.

As such, the length of time taken to draft, score and then revise these Psalms is reflective of Britten's more thoroughgoing and considered practice while at college, honed after several years' tuition with Frank Bridge and refined further as a student. After the initial drafts in July and October 1931, the psalms were revised, orchestrated and then re-orchestrated (in the case of Psalm 130), and neither piece was finalised until January 1932. Along with Ireland, Herbert Howells also contributed comments and suggestions, and the pieces were championed by none other than Ralph Vaughan Williams, who endeavoured over several months to get them performed. Vaughan Williams was unsuccessful, despite his best efforts, and they were never in fact performed in Britten's lifetime, possibly due to the large forces required. It was not until the later 1930s that Britten composed again on such a large scale, and these pieces—for example, *King Arthur* and *Ballad of Heroes*—were commissioned especially for radio broadcast.

The orchestration and the configuration of the choral parts look at first glance surprisingly traditional, perhaps especially given that the more definitive and adventurous *Sinfonietta* (op. 1) was only six months away. The nuanced melancholy flavour of the first psalm, however, already looks forward to the soundworld of *A Boy Was Born* (op. 3), Britten's highly-regarded choral work of 1933; the pulsating energy and bustle of the second piece, the melodic fragments racing across all instruments and vocal parts, represent Britten's love of playful syncopation and driving rhythms that were to remain characteristic of his music. It should also be remembered that these pieces were written by a still very young composer: Britten was a mere 17 when he completed the early drafts, and 18 when he finished the orchestrations.

In May 1932 Britten submitted them, along with the Phantasy Quintet in F minor (Jan-Feb 1932), in support of his application for the Mendelssohn Scholarship at the Royal College of Music: the application was unsuccessful, although he was awarded £50 by the scholarship committee in order not to 'discourage' him from composing. He was successful in his subsequent year's application to the Scholarship Committee, so it seems the £50 served its purpose; and of course the rest is a highly successful history. Britten revisited the text of Psalm 150 years later in 1962, by which stage nothing he composed would have struggled to be performed.

Dr Lucy Walker
Director of Learning and Development,
Britten-Pears Foundation

I – PSALM 130
(Out of the deep)

BENJAMIN BRITTEN

poco più agitato

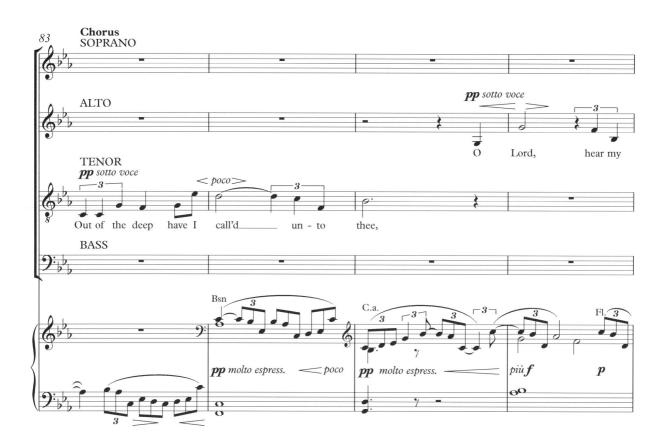

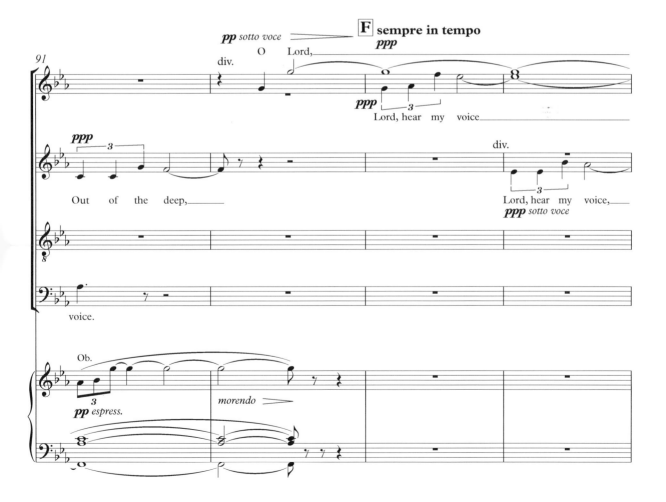

14

G **poco più allegro**
SOPRANO SOLO (from the Chorus)

For there is mer-cy with thee: there - fore shalt thou be fear'd.

I look for the Lord; my soul doth wait for him: in his

Lord, hear my voice. Lord, hear my

Lord, hear my voice,

Lord, hear my voice. Lord, hear my

Lord, hear my voice,

word is my trust. My soul fle-eth un-to the Lord: be-fore the morn - ing watch, I say,

voice, Lord, hear my voice, Lord, hear my voice, Lord, hear my

Lord, hear my voice, Lord, hear my voice, Lord, hear my voice, Lord,

voice, Lord, hear my voice, Lord, hear my voice, Lord, hear my

Lord, hear my voice, Lord, hear my voice, Lord, hear my voice, Lord,

Ob./C.a.

più allegro e vivace

I Risoluto

-tion,____ is plent-eous re-demp - tion.

-tion, is plent-eous re-demp - tion,____ re - demp - tion.

-demp - tion, with him is plent-eous re-demp - tion.

plent-eous re-demp - tion, plent - eous re-demp - tion.

J **più maestoso**

And he shall re - deem Is - ra - el: from all his

poco più lento

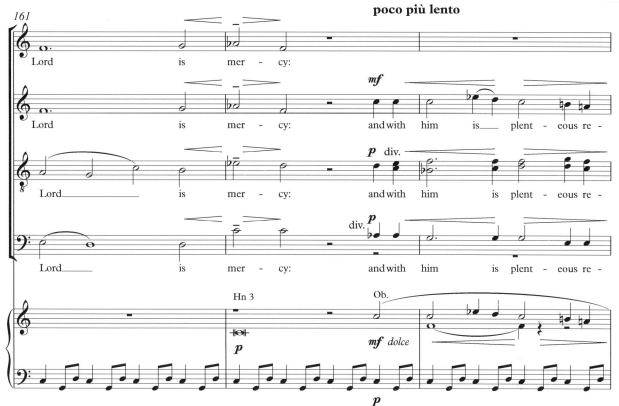

Lord is mer - cy:

Lord is mer - cy: and with him is plent - eous re -

Lord is mer - cy: and with him is plent - eous re -

Lord is mer - cy: and with him is plent - eous re -

Hn 3   Ob.

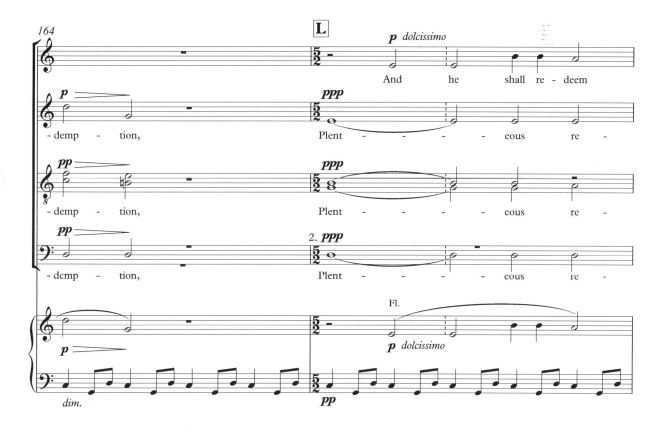

L

And he shall re - deem

- demp - tion, Plent - - - eous re -

- demp - tion, Plent - - - eous re -

- demp - tion, Plent - - - eous re -

Fl.

dim.

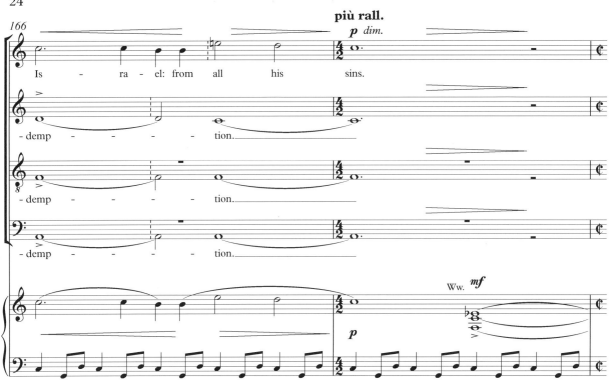

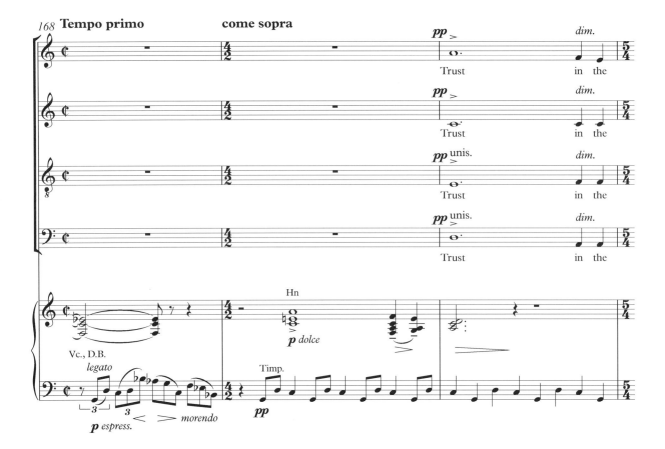

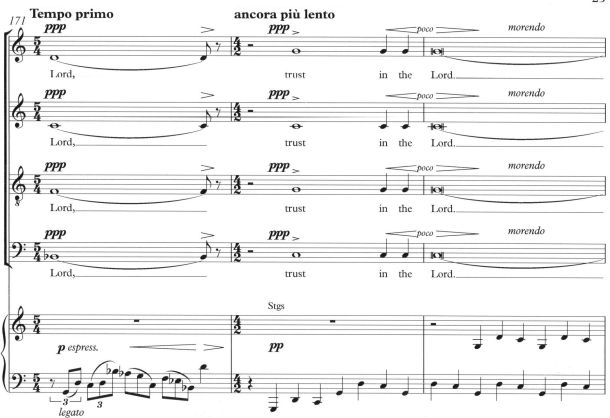

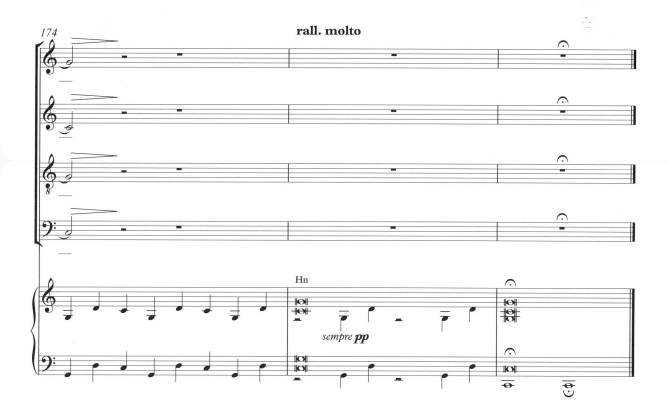

II – PSALM 150
(Praise ye the Lord)

BENJAMIN BRITTEN

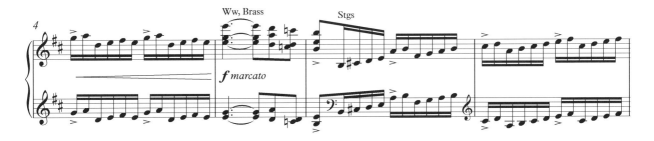

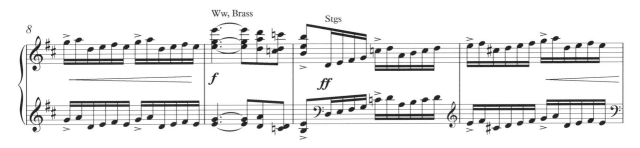

praise——— ye the Lord.
praise——— ye the Lord.
praise——— ye the Lord.
praise——— ye the Lord.

sempre **ff**

div. ***f***
Praise,———

ff
Praise——— ye the Lord.——

div. ***f***
Praise,———

ff
Praise——— ye the Lord.——

Stgs

f

ff

praise___ ye the Lord, praise,___ praise.

praise___ ye the Lord, praise,___ praise.

praise___ ye the Lord, praise,___ praise.

praise___ ye the Lord, praise,___ praise.

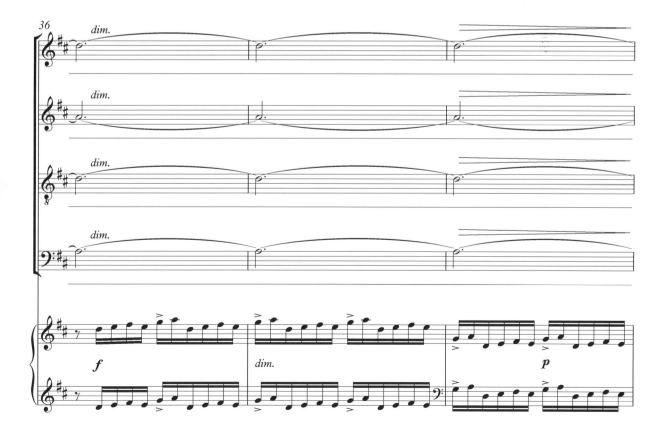

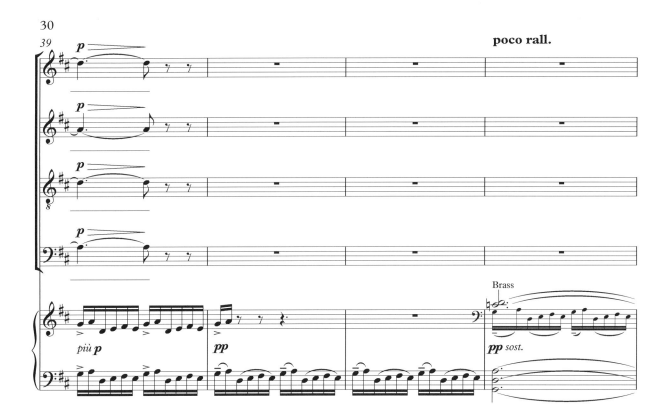

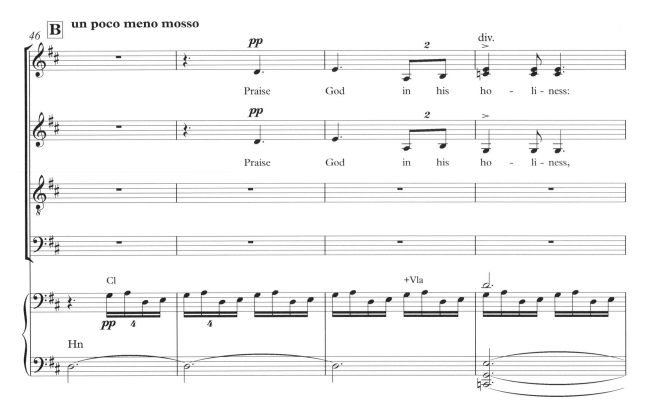

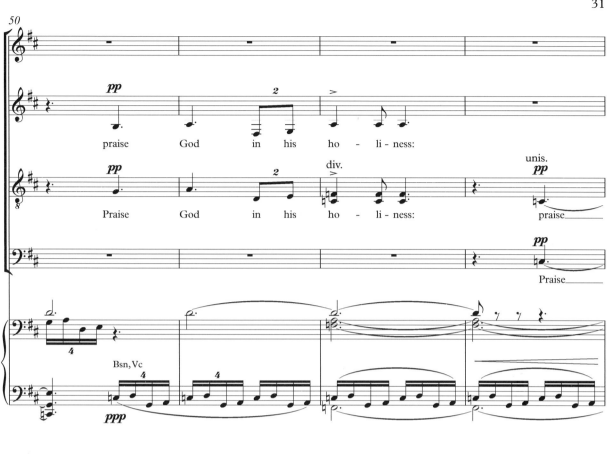

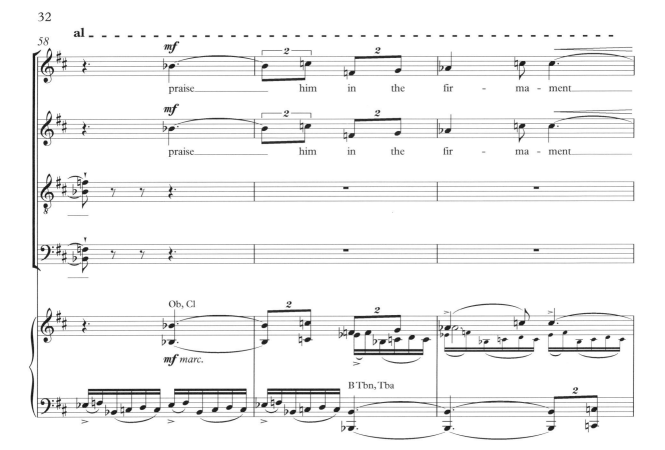

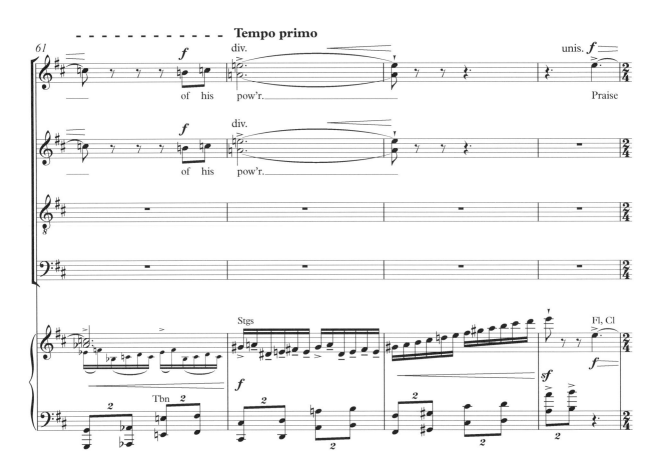

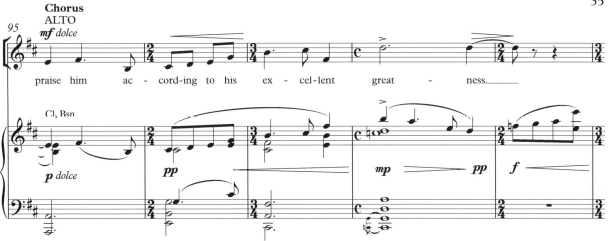

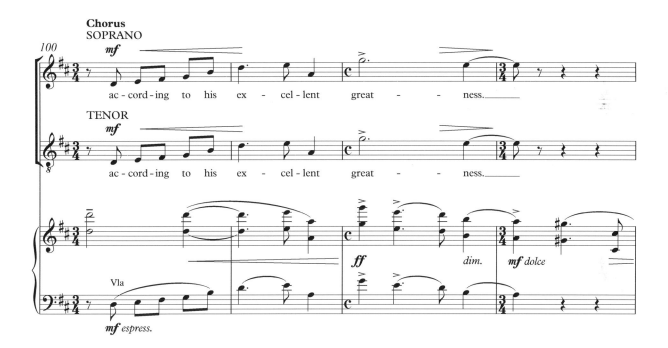

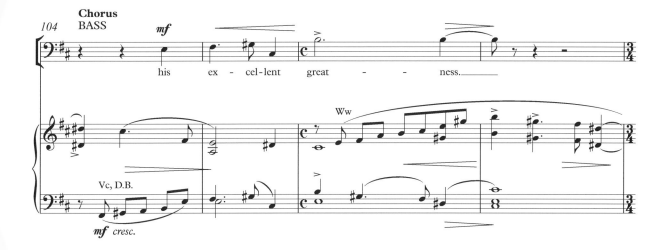

Praise him___ in the cym - bals and

Praise him___ in the cym - bals and

dan - ces,

dan - ces,

135

praise him____ in the cym - - bals and dan - - ces:

praise him____ in the cym - - bals and dan - - ces:

Snare Drum

Vln

139

praise_____ him____ up-on the strings

praise_____ him____ up-on the strings

Hn

sim.

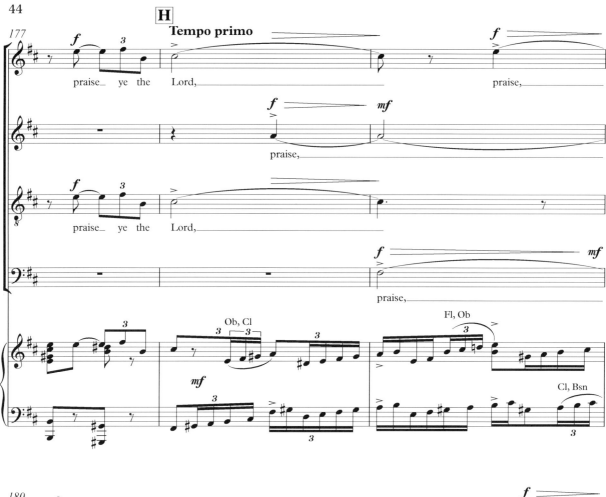

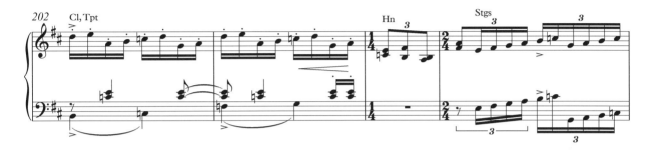

allargando al fine